ESTES ADESIVOS COMPÕEM O *COUNTING GAME* (JOGO DE CONTAR) E DEVEM SER COLADOS NA CAPA DO LIVRO PARA COMPLETAR A QUANTIDADE CORRETA DE FIGURAS.

ELIETE CANESI MORINO • RITA BRUGIN DE FARIA

EDUCAÇÃO INFANTIL

editora ática

CONTENTS

ACOMPANHA ESTE LIVRO O *READER* **MAG, THE OWL**.

WELCOME! 3	**UNIT 7** – DAY BY DAY 31	**CELEBRATION CRAFTS** 55
UNIT 1 – MY FAMILY 7	**UNIT 8** – TIME TO EAT 35	**THE SONG BOOK** 67
UNIT 2 – MY FAVORITE TOYS 11	**UNIT 9** – A BEAUTIFUL DAY 39	**PICTURE DICTIONARY** 69
UNIT 3 – MY CLASSROOM 15	**UNIT 10** – FARM ANIMALS 43	**STICKERS** 73
UNIT 4 – IS IT BIG OR SMALL? 19	**UNIT 11** – MY BODY 47	**GAMES** 77
UNIT 5 – COLORS AND SHAPES 23	**UNIT 12** – THE WEATHER 51	**MINI-CARDS** 85
UNIT 6 – NUMBERS 27		

ICONS

 CIRCLE
 COLOR
 COUNT
 CUT
 DOT TO DOT
 DRAW
 GLUE
 INTERNET
 LET'S TALK

 LISTEN AND SAY
 MAKE AN X
 MATCH
 NUMBER
 POINT
 PRINT
 SING OR CHANT
 STICK

LOOK AND CIRCLE.

FIND 4 DIFFERENCES.

GROWING UP

 LET'S TALK!

 SING AND DRAW.

 RESPECT!

HELLO, MY NAME IS

_____

UNIT 1 — MY FAMILY

 LISTEN AND STICK.

MATCH.

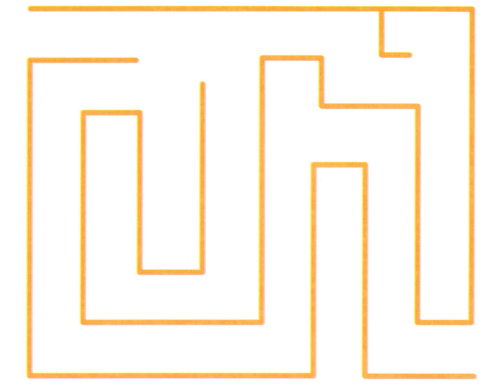

GROWING UP

 LET'S TALK!

 SING AND DRAW.

 BE POLITE!

LISTEN AND COLOR.

 MATCH.

GROWING UP

 LET'S TALK!

 SING AND GLUE.

CARE FOR TOYS!

LISTEN, DOT TO DOT AND COLOR.

MATCH.

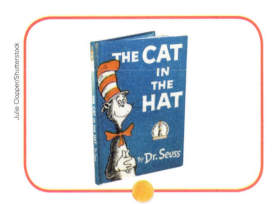

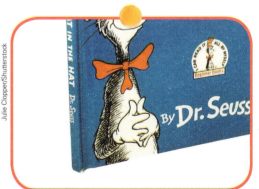

GROWING UP

 LET'S TALK!

 SING AND STICK.

BE FRIENDLY!

  # LISTEN AND CIRCLE.

 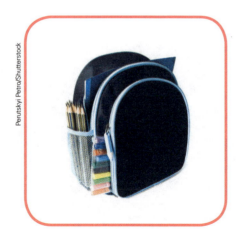  

STICK.

MAKE AN X.

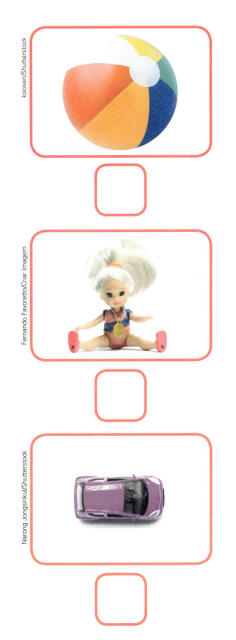

GROWING UP

 LET'S TALK!

 SING AND DOT TO DOT.

SOLIDARITY!

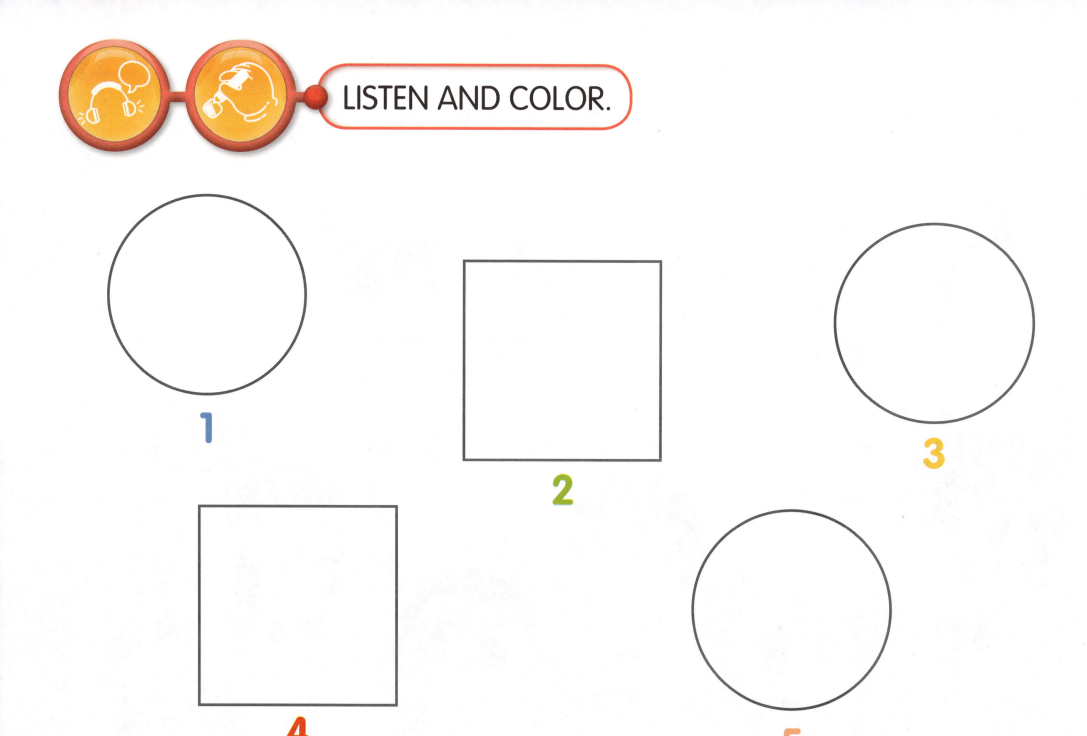

MATCH THE BALLOONS!

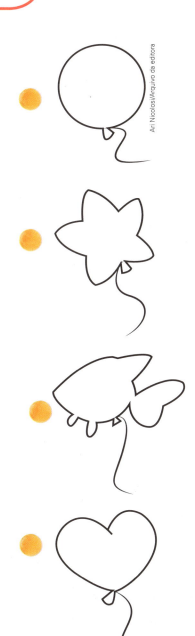

COMPLETE THE DRAWING.

GROWING UP

 LET'S TALK!

 SING AND STICK.

BE CAREFUL!

LISTEN AND COLOR.

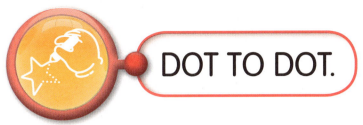 DOT TO DOT.

 DRAW.

6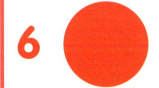

4

5

GROWING UP

 LET'S TALK.

 SING AND STICK.

 BE NICE, SHARE!

LISTEN AND MATCH.

STICK.

LOOK AND CIRCLE.

 ➡

 ➡

 ➡

 ➡

GROWING UP

 LET'S TALK.

 SING AND MATCH.

 **BODY CARE!**

LISTEN AND COLOR.

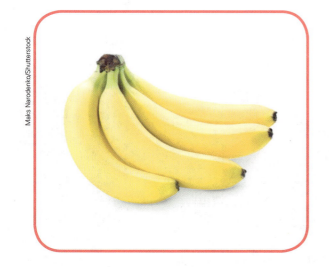

 CIRCLE THE ODD ONE OUT.

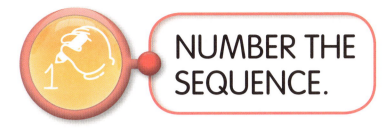 NUMBER THE SEQUENCE.

GROWING UP

 LET'S TALK!

 SING AND DOT TO DOT.

HEALTHY HABITS!

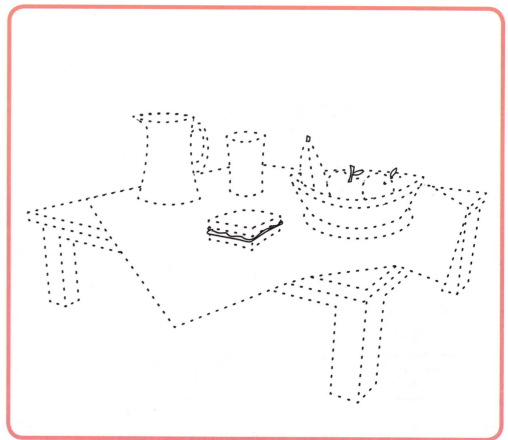

LISTEN, STICK AND DRAW.

 DRAW AND COLOR.

  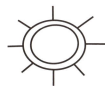

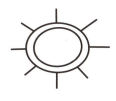

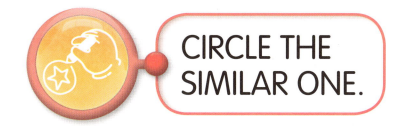 CIRCLE THE SIMILAR ONE.

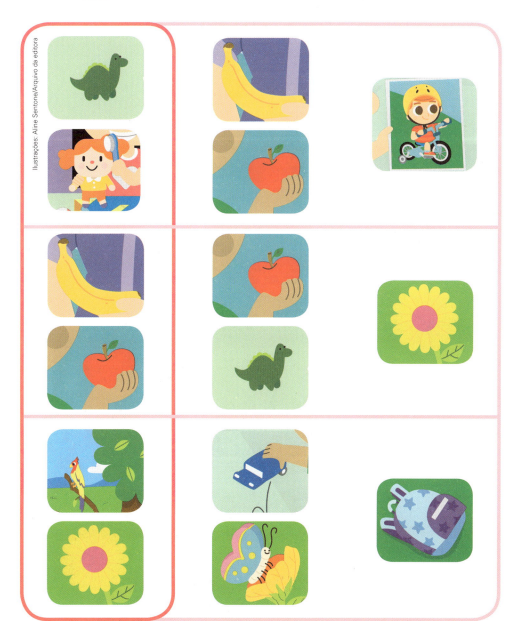

GROWING UP

 LET'S TALK!

 SING AND COLOR.

RESPECT NATURE!

  LISTEN AND MAKE AN X.

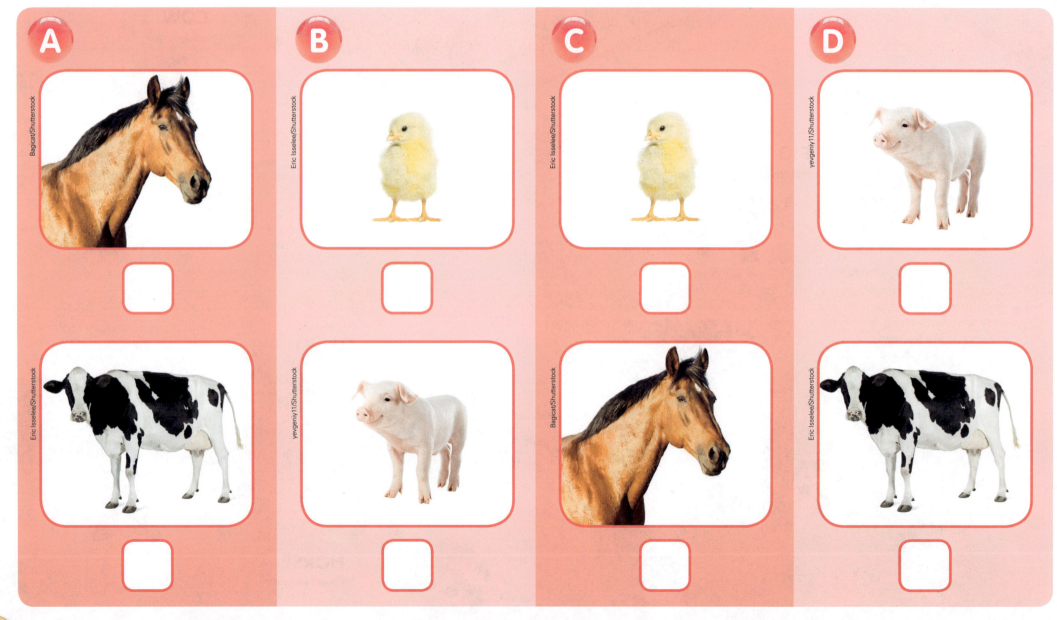

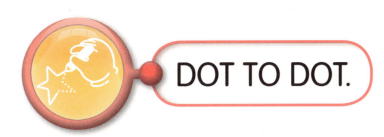 DOT TO DOT.

 LOOK AND COUNT.

GROWING UP

 LET'S TALK!

 SING AND CIRCLE.

RESPECT THE ANIMALS!

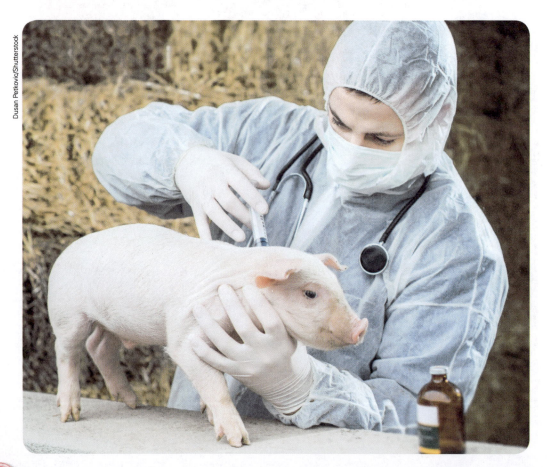

STICK AND COMPLETE.

 DOT TO DOT AND COLOR.

 MATCH THE JIGSAW.

GROWING UP

 LET'S TALK!

  SING AND DRAW.

 HEALTH!

LISTEN AND COLOR.

MATCH.

MAKE AN X AND DRAW.

GROWING UP

 LET'S TALK!

RESPECT THE ENVIRONMENT

 SING AND MATCH.

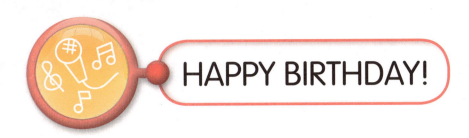

HAPPY BIRTHDAY!

HAPPY BIRTHDAY TO YOU!

HAPPY BIRTHDAY TO YOU!

HAPPY BIRTHDAY, DEAR CAROL!

HAPPY BIRTHDAY TO YOU!

HAPPY EASTER!

EASTER BUNNY

EASTER BUNNY,

EASTER BUNNY,

WHAT DO YOU BRING TO ME?

ONE EGG, TWO EGGS, THREE EGGS, SO, SO!

ONE EGG, TWO EGGS, THREE EGGS, SO, SO!

HAPPY MOTHER'S DAY!

MOTHER'S DAY

ROSES ARE RED,
VIOLETS ARE BLUE,
SUGAR IS SWEET
AND SO ARE YOU!

HAPPY FATHER'S DAY!

DEAR, DAD!

OH ME! OH MY!

OH MY! OH ME!

IF ANYBODY LOVES DAD,

IT'S ME! IT'S ME! IT'S ME!

YOU'RE MY HERO

THANKSGIVING DAY

MR. TURKEY

MR. TURKEY, MR. TURKEY!

RUN AWAY, RUN AWAY!

PLEASE, BE CAREFUL!

[...]

IT'S THANKSGIVING DAY!

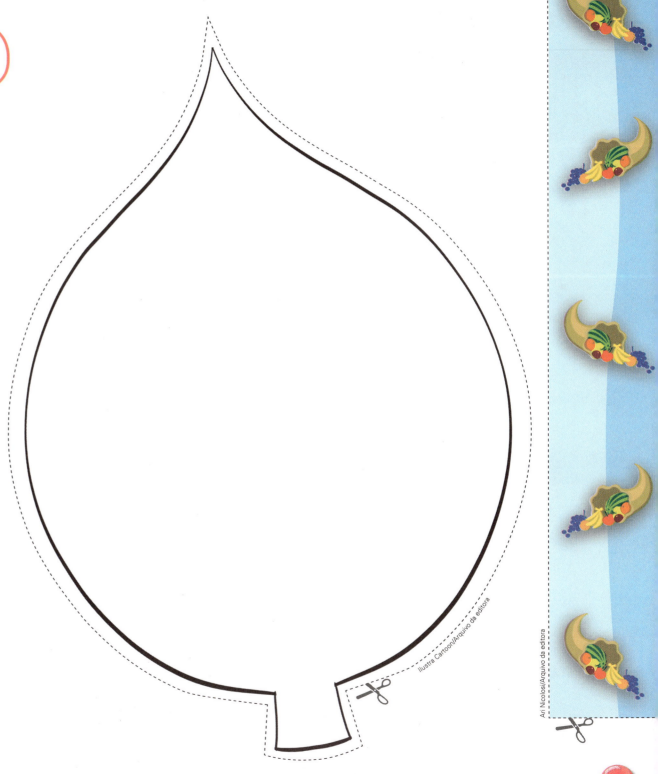

MERRY CHRISTMAS!

WE WISH YOU A MERRY CHRISTMAS!

WE WISH YOU A MERRY CHRISTMAS.
WE WISH YOU A MERRY CHRISTMAS.
WE WISH YOU A MERRY CHRISTMAS,
AND A HAPPY NEW YEAR!

THE SONG BOOK

PICTURE DICTIONARY

STICKERS

PAGE 6

NAME
_____

NAME
_____

NAME
_____

PAGE 8

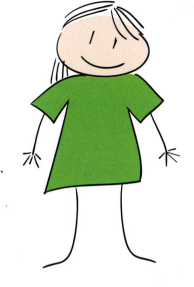

PAGE 3 - READER

PAGE 18

PAGE 26

PAGE 21

PAGE 33

PAGE 30

5 1 3

PAGE 40

PAGE 48

76

MEMORY GAME

DRINK	**DRINK**	**EAT**	**EAT**

PLAY	**PLAY**	**SLEEP**	**SLEEP**

HAPPY	**HAPPY**	**SAD**	**SAD**

BIG BALL	**BIG BALL**	**SMALL BALL**	**SMALL BALL**

FAMILY PUZZLE

FAMILY AND TEACHER PUPPETS

NUMBERS GAME

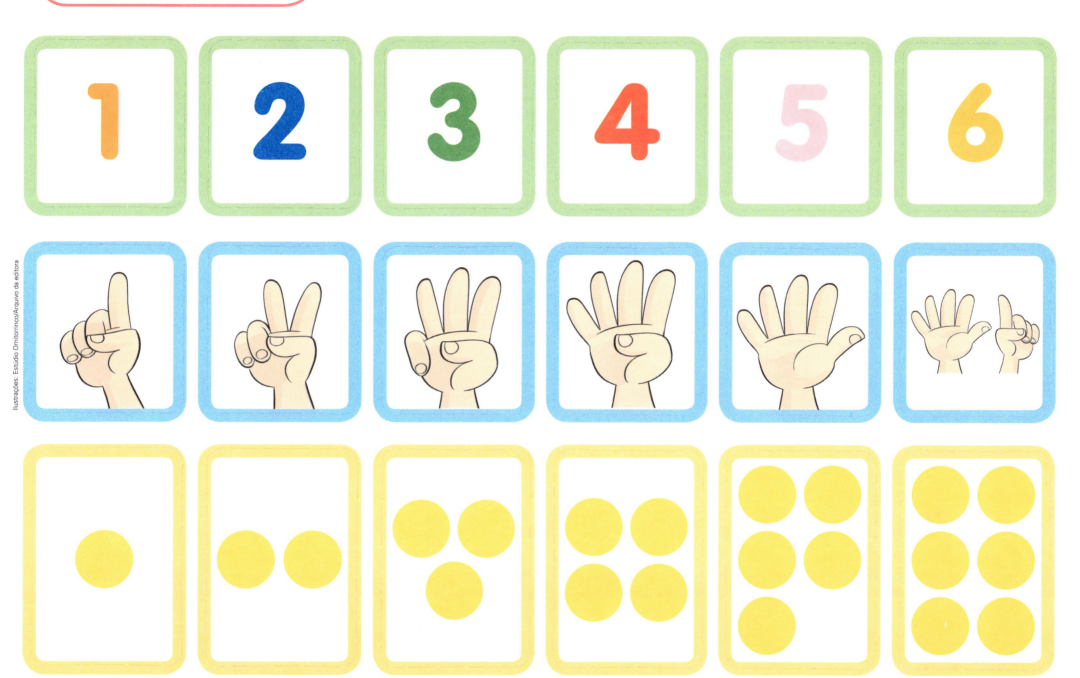

TIME TO EAT AND FAVORITE TOYS

THE WEATHER AND MY CLASSROOM

COLORS, SHAPES AND THE WEATHER

FARM ANIMALS AND MY BODY

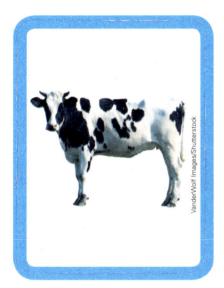

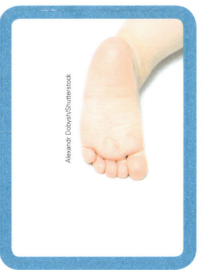